Origins

Air Scare

Jan Burchett and Sara Vogler ▪ Jonatronix

OXFORD
UNIVERSITY PRESS

The Whizzer

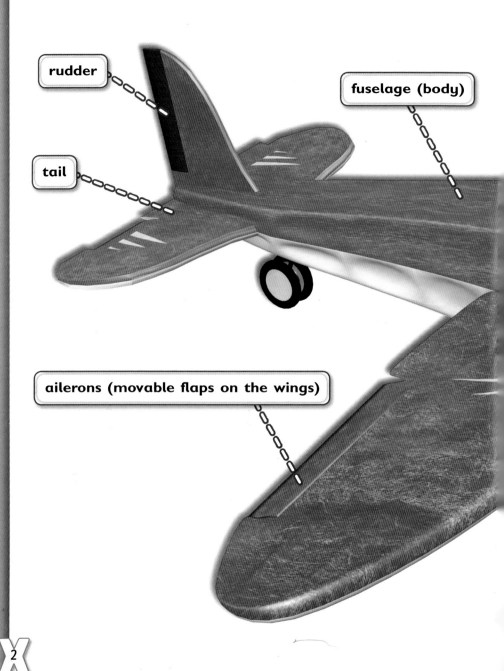

rudder

fuselage (body)

tail

ailerons (movable flaps on the wings)

wing

cockpit

propeller

wheel

Max and Tiger made their way through the crowd at
the school gates. Tiger was carefully carrying a remote-
control aeroplane. The school had been doing a project
on flight all term and some children had made their
own planes. Tiger was particularly proud of his. He'd
called it the Whizzer.

Now everyone was gathering on this sunny Saturday
afternoon to see the planes in action. Mrs Mills, the
head teacher, was going to judge which plane did the
best display. The prize was some tickets to an air show.

"Did I tell you about the Whizzer?" beamed Tiger.

"Yes," said Max, "you did." *Karla*

"It's got a fifty centimetre wingspan," Tiger went on.

"You told me," smiled Max. *Npo*

Tiger pointed to the bit sticking up at the end of the tail. "It's got a fully working rudder ... and ailerons on the wings. That all makes it easy to steer."

"You told me that as well!" joked Max. "Twice."

"... and look at the streamlined fuselage." *Tuesday*

"OK, Tiger," grinned Max. "It's the best plane ever."

Max looked around the crowd.

"Oh, no!" he said, with a shudder. "There's Lucy. Why did *she* have to come?"

Lucy was always causing trouble. As she walked across the school field, Max could see that she was carrying something large and lumpy in a bag.

"She did make a plane for the project," shrugged Tiger, "but it was rubbish. I can't believe she'd enter that."

"I wonder what she's got in the bag then?" said Max.

"Who cares," said Tiger. "I'm going to practise.
I have to launch the plane into the wind to lift it up
into the air."

He checked which way the wind was blowing and
turned his plane to face it. Then he switched it on.
It hummed into life. Next, Tiger turned on the
remote control.

The Whizzer ran along the ground, slowly at first
and then faster and faster. Tiger pressed gently on the
up button and the plane rose into the air to join the
others that were buzzing around the sky.

"Wow!" breathed Max. "Smooth take-off!"

"That's nothing," said Tiger. "Watch this!"

The Whizzer climbed steeply and then, to Max's amazement, flipped over backwards and made a complete circle.

"Cool!" gasped Max. "A loop-the-loop."

"I've got plenty more tricks for the competition," Tiger grinned.

Then all of a sudden Tiger was knocked to one side. He nearly lost control of his plane.

Chapter 2 - Cheating in the air

"Move over!" said a loud voice. "Give me some room!"

It was Lucy. She elbowed Tiger out of the way and bent down, carefully putting her lumpy bag on the ground. Then she undid it to reveal a sleek, gleaming model plane. Long blue ribbons hung from the tail.

"Make way for the Air Shark!" she announced.

The Air Shark

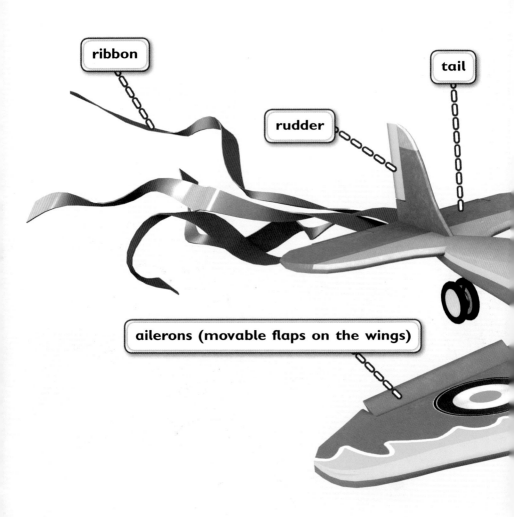

ribbon

tail

rudder

ailerons (movable flaps on the wings)

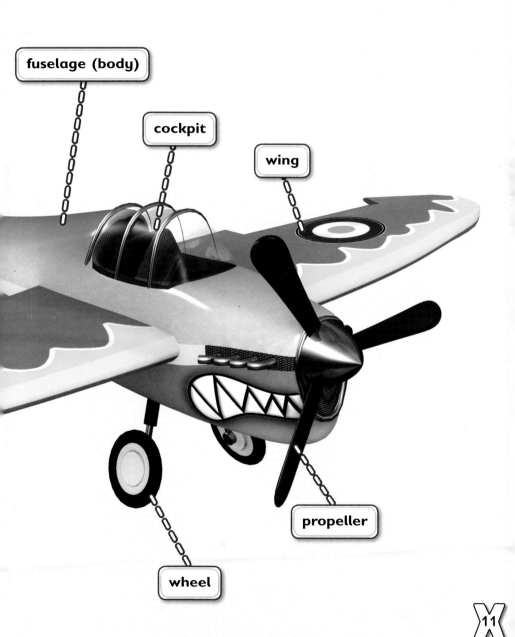

fuselage (body)

cockpit

wing

propeller

wheel

Max nudged Tiger. "You said her plane was useless," he whispered.

Tiger had just about managed to regain control of the Whizzer. He snatched a quick look at the Air Shark. "It *was* useless!" he muttered. "That's not the same plane."

Max checked the competitors' board where ten names were written. "Well, whether it's hers or not she's entered the competition."

Flying Competition

1. Katie
2. Jamal
3. Leo
4. Hope
5. Jack
6. Bella
7. Asif
8. Mei
9. Lucy
10. Tiger

Max could see that Tiger was getting agitated.

"Never mind," he said quickly. "You're last, after Lucy. You'll have seen all the others, so you'll know who you have to beat."

"Maybe," said Tiger, doubtfully.

"Watch this, everyone!" said Lucy loudly.

She launched the Air Shark into the wind. It sped
up into the sky, engine roaring. It looked as if it could
do some amazing tricks. But instead, Lucy steered
it straight for a bright yellow plane that was in the
middle of a roll.

SMASH! The Air Shark crashed into the side of the
yellow plane. It didn't stand a chance. It plummeted to
the ground in a spiral.

"Whoops!" tittered Lucy. "Sorry."

Lucy's fingers flew over her remote control, sending the Air Shark into a steep dive.

It bashed against a small biplane and snapped the propeller off! The plane dropped on to the school roof.

"Silly me!" said Lucy with a nasty grin. "I'm not very good at steering."

"Don't let her get near the Whizzer," Max whispered to Tiger.

Tiger pressed his steering button hard to the right and the Air Shark went speeding past.

"Phew!" said Max. "That was close!"

Then the Air Shark made a quick U-turn.

"Watch out!" shouted Max.

It was too late.

BANG! The Air Shark had done a fast turn and slammed into the Whizzer.

Horrified, Max and Tiger watched the Whizzer tumble from the sky. It crashed into the long grass at the edge of the playing field.

Chapter 3 - The search

Lucy landed the Air Shark and began to smooth out its ribbons, as if she hadn't done anything wrong.

"You've broken my plane!" Tiger shouted. He was about to run over to her but Max caught his arm.

"There's no time," he said. "We've got to find the Whizzer. It might still fly."

Max and Tiger ran towards the edge of the playing field where they had seen the plane crash-land. They hunted up and down among the tangled grass but could not find the Whizzer anywhere.

"ATTENTION PLEASE!" A voice boomed out from the loudspeaker. "THE GRAND FLYING COMPETITION IS ABOUT TO START."

They heard a buzz of excitement from the crowd. All the other competitors made their way to the judge's table.

"Oh, no!" wailed Tiger, as the first plane took to the air. "They're starting!"

Just then, Max's foot touched something hard. He looked down. It was the Whizzer.

"Here it is," he yelled, pulling it out of the grass.

Tiger inspected his plane. The shiny red fuselage was all scratched and scraped.

"Look what Lucy's done!" he wailed.

"Never mind that," said Max, firmly. "Does it work?"

Tiger flicked the switch on the plane. Nothing happened.

"She *has* broken it," he cried. "I'm out of the competition and it's all her fault."

Chapter 4 – Max has a plan

Max had never seen Tiger so upset.

"Don't give up now," he said. "I'm sure we can get the Whizzer working."

Tiger lifted up a panel on the side of the plane, near the cockpit, and peered inside. "I can't see anything wrong."

"Check the battery," suggested Max.

Tiger poked his fingers inside the small space.

"That's it! One of the wires has come loose. There isn't any power."

"Can you fix it?" asked Max.

Tiger tried to prise the battery out. "No, it's stuck."

Max thought fast.

"I know," he said. "I'll shrink and fix it for you. You hold the remote and get ready. As soon as I've finished I'll jump clear and you can take off."

"Great plan, Max!" said Tiger gratefully. "You'll be able to reach the wires better from inside the cockpit."

Tiger carried the plane back to the edge of the playground and put it down facing the wind ready for take-off. Max checked to make sure no one was looking. Luckily everyone's eyes were on the display in the air.

Max turned the dial on his watch. He pushed the X and ...

Micro-Max climbed up the side of the Whizzer and in through the cockpit hatch.

Tiger heard everyone clapping as another plane finished its display.

"Hurry up, Max!" he whispered. "It'll be my turn soon."

Chapter 5 - Take-off!

Max crawled to the back of the plane on his hands and knees. He grasped the loose wire in both hands and began to pull. It took all his strength to bend it towards the battery terminal.

Time was running out. The Air Shark had taken off. That meant Tiger would be next. Tiger watched as Lucy made the Air Shark twist and turn in the sky, blue ribbons streaming behind. Then she brought it down low over everyone's heads, making it release a plume of smoke. It was going to be hard to beat.

Inside the cockpit of the Whizzer, Max was still trying to bend the wire back towards the battery terminal. He sat down so he could put all his weight into it. Suddenly, there was a satisfying click and ... *VROOM, VROOM, WHIRR!* The plane burst into life.

"Oh, no!" said Max. "Tiger must have forgotten to flick the plane's OFF switch."

The plane began to move.

Max scrambled towards the front of the cockpit. He was about to climb out and jump clear when the front of the plane tipped up. The plane began to take off. Max slid back and the cockpit hatch slammed closed.

"Tiger, help!" he yelled.

But Tiger couldn't hear him with all the noise from the cheering crowd. He didn't even know the plane had taken off. He was too busy watching the Air Shark.

"Help!" shouted Max again, desperately.

Chapter 6 - Out of control

"Did you see that, Max?" asked Tiger. "Lucy will be hard to beat." Tiger looked over his shoulder, down at the ground. "Max?"

Then he looked up.

"Oh, no!" he said, as he saw the Whizzer climbing into the sky. He quickly picked up the remote control and moved the joystick. The Whizzer was not responding.

The Whizzer climbed higher and higher. Max stumbled to the front of the plane.

He crawled into the plastic seat and strapped himself in.

Meanwhile, down on the ground, Tiger was desperately fiddling with the remote control. He could not get it to work at all. He was not worried about the competition now. He was just worried about getting Max down safely.

Lucy, on the other hand, was very pleased with her performance. She turned smugly to the crowd.

"Competition's over," she announced. "Guess who's the winner?"

She was about to land the Air Shark when she saw the Whizzer appear over the trees. Her smile froze.

"I thought I'd got rid of that one," she muttered. "I'll show *him*."

She turned the Air Shark expertly round.

Chapter 7 – Captain Max

Up in the air, the Whizzer had levelled out. Max looked out of the window and gulped. It was a very long way down. From up here, everyone and everything looked micro-sized. He hoped that Tiger would land the plane soon.

It was then he saw the Air Shark, heading straight towards him.

"Tiger will make the plane turn in a minute," Max said to himself confidently.

The Whizzer carried on in a straight path. There was something wrong.

"Tiger must have lost control!" yelled Max. "I'm going to crash!"

Max had to do something. He grabbed the joystick in front of him.

"This had better work," he said through gritted teeth. He slammed the joystick to the left.

The plane tilted wildly and swerved away from the Air Shark, missing it by millimetres.

"Manual control!" he said. "Great!"

He pushed the joystick forwards. The plane dived. He pulled it towards him – the plane soared back up into the air. He flew the plane out over the trees.

Max was just beginning to enjoy himself when he heard a name being called over the loudspeaker. It was Tiger's. He had to get back. They had a competition to win.

Tiger breathed a sigh of relief when he saw his plane appearing over the tree tops again. The Whizzer dived down and skimmed over his head. He caught sight of a tiny figure giving him a thumbs-up from the cockpit. It was Max!

"Well, there's nothing in the rules that says that I can't have a micro-pilot!" beamed Tiger.

Chapter 8 - Max to the rescue

Lucy landed the Air Shark. She looked over at Mrs Mills and the other judges. Their eyes were all now fixed on the Whizzer.

"That's it," Lucy thought. "I'm going to make sure the Whizzer has had its last flight!"

Lucy crept up to Tiger and grabbed at the remote control in his hands. Tiger held on to it tightly. There was a terrible tussle.

Up in the plane, Max saw his friend struggling to keep hold of the remote control. He pushed the joystick forwards as hard as he could and dived.

"Right, Lucy," he muttered to himself. "You're in for a surprise!"

Lucy finally wrenched the remote control out of Tiger's hands. She pushed hard on the down button.

"Bye bye, Whizzer," she smirked.

But the Whizzer didn't crash into the ground as she had expected. Instead, it flew straight at her. With an ear-piercing scream she turned and ran ...

Aaaaggghhh!

Wherever Lucy went the Whizzer followed her, buzzing around her like an angry bee. Finally she ran over to the judge's table. The Whizzer zoomed away into the air. Lucy threw the remote control down.

"It wasn't me," she said, red in the face. "I didn't do anything!"

"I think you've done quite enough, Lucy," said Mrs Mills sternly. "You are disqualified from the competition!"

Tiger picked up the remote control from the ground where Lucy had thrown it. He pretended to press the buttons again. He knew it was up to Max to finish the display.

The crowd gasped as Max made the Whizzer roll and dive and whoosh low over their heads, then spin upside down. Everyone laughed and clapped.

"Go, Max," whispered Tiger, excitedly.

"And now to finish with a loop-the-loop!" said Max confidently. He pulled the joystick. The plane rose steeply until it was vertical, nose pointing to the sky.

Then Max felt the plane tip over on to its back.
He hung in his seat as the world turned upside down.

The Whizzer flipped right over. It was a perfect loop-the-loop!

Max brought the plane down and landed smoothly on the playground.

The loudspeaker crackled into life. "THE WINNER OF THE GRAND FLYING COMPETITION IS ... TIGER," it announced.

Tiger picked up the Whizzer and found himself surrounded by children jostling to congratulate him. Mrs Mills beckoned him forwards and gave him his prize of the air show tickets. Everyone cheered and clapped.

Finally Tiger escaped the crowd. He sneaked off behind the school and put the plane down.

Max staggered out of the cockpit and flopped to the ground, exhausted but happy. Then he turned the dial on his watch and grew back to normal size.

"Thank you, Max," grinned Tiger. "You were great!" He held out the air show tickets. "You'll come with me, won't you? You deserve it. There'll be displays and models and we get a ride in a real helicopter."

"Of course I'll come," said Max. "Maybe I can show them a few tricks!"

Find out more ...

To find out more about heroes and villains read ...

Heroine in Hiding

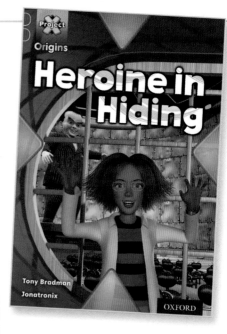

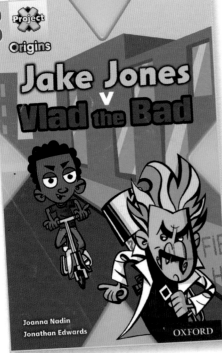

and *Jake Jones v Vlad the Bad*